Good Bosses Gone Bad

Good Bosses Gone Bad

How to Survive the Workplace When Your Boss Sucks!

April Boyd-Noronha, MBA

authorHOUSE®

AuthorHouse™
1663 Liberty Drive
Bloomington, IN 47403
www.authorhouse.com
Phone: 1-800-839-8640

First published by AuthorHouse 01/27/2012

ISBN: 978-1-4685-3962-2 (sc)
ISBN: 978-1-4685-3961-5 (ebk)

Library of Congress Control Number: 2012900011

Printed in the United States of America

Any people depicted in stock imagery provided by Thinkstock are models, and such images are being used for illustrative purposes only.
Certain stock imagery © Thinkstock.

This book is printed on acid-free paper.

Because of the dynamic nature of the Internet, any web addresses or links contained in this book may have changed since publication and may no longer be valid. The views expressed in this work are solely those of the author and do not necessarily reflect the views of the publisher, and the publisher hereby disclaims any responsibility for them.

Author's note: This book is not intended to provide medical advice or to take the place of medical advice treatment from your personal physician. Readers are advised to consult their own doctors or other qualified health professional regarding the treatment of their medical conditions. Neither the publisher nor the author takes any responsibility for any possible consequences from following the information in this book.

Back cover photo by Andres Nelson

CONTENTS

I dedicate this book to every employee and supervisor who is or has been:

Frustrated with upper management

A member of the "working poor" class

Laid off or had their job eliminated

Holding on until the next/better job presents itself

At the brink of breaking down

Tired of the consistent incompetence of their boss

Trying to do the right thing even when the wrong thing is being done to them

Underutilized

Undervalued

Overlooked

Overworked

Acknowledgments

With special thanks:

To my children—Zaria, Nyah, and Caleb. I know you all understand why Mommy had to take the time (away from you) to finish this project. Once this book is published, I pray that it will be the catalyst to enable me to spend more time with you.

To my Mommy, Clarissa. There is no amount of words to express how I feel. But if I had to, here are a few: momma, best friend, confidante, counselor, encourager, voice of reason . . . the list goes on and on. As a single parent, you held it down. Look at me now! I'm still trying to be half the woman you have always shown me to be. I'm glad God allowed you to share with me yet another pivotal moment of my life.

To my posse—Val, Tamara, Kelly, Robin, LaVerne, Wanda, Suzanne, and Keith & Trecie. Each of you has encouraged me in your own special way. It may have been a phone call, text, email, word of encouragement, or a simple prayer. One thing for sure, EVERY time I reached out to you, you were there. I owe you one my faithful friends.

To Andres Nelson, my photographer. We've just met, but it's amazing how you saw in me what I didn't see. We were pressed for time, but you made it work. I still can't believe that the last shot, was THE one! I am glad to now also call you "friend". So, you know what that means—you have been forewarned.

To Cierra Haynes, my stylist. For every (and I mean every) time you had to drag me into the salon to do my hair—I thank you. You make me look good!

Last, but not least, to all my former bad bosses. This book definitely could not have been written without your many negative encounters and comments, consistent incompetence, and blatant lack of moral judgment during my years of employment with you.

April Boyd-Noronha, MBA

"The Retail Trainer"

Introduction

I can vividly recall the day I realized that I had a "good boss gone bad". I reflected on our initial conversations that were filled with such words of encouragement. The first few encounters were truly bonding moments that I felt would be a firm foundation for further mentoring. But I came to understand that it all was a façade that soon came tumbling down as my workload increased seemingly overnight, my stress level soared though the roof, and I just couldn't seem to keep up!

I quickly had to assess my current situation. Let me see here. Years of experience in customer service in various industries—check! Undergraduate degree in business management <u>and</u> an MBA—check! High level of integrity where I always try to do the right thing—check! Firm belief in the good of my fellow man/woman—check! Hard working, always willing to go the extra mile—check! Never fail to roll up my sleeves to help my team—check! So, what was wrong with this picture? Wait a minute. Was it me OR was it my boss?!

Bad Bosses Gone Bad is by no means an exhaustive commentary. Instead it was written with the intention of being used as a handy, user-friendly, easy-to-read reference book. By utilizing these practical tools and insights designed to help you survive within a office where bad bosses reign, you will be able to masterfully excel and penetrate the pinnacle of incompetence that occupies the offices of your workplace.

How to Use This Book

By effectively utilizing this practical tool you will gain an insight into the dynamics that exist within today's workplace between bad bosses and those who report to them. I suggest you start by taking the quiz (see page xv) to better determine whether you actually report to a bad boss or simply a boss that is learning the ropes and needs time to adjust and adapt to a new working environment. I caution you to not fall into the trap of taking the easy route, merely categorizing your boss as a "good boss gone bad". This will not help workplace relations and will further delay the progress needed at your workplace.

Once you identify the character traits of your boss, you will be well on your way to determining how best to counteract these "bad boss" traits in an effort to survive the demise of your department or collapse of a company. This book has been designed to give you hope while working in a seemingly hopeless workplace that is led by a bad boss. I challenge you to allow this book to empower you—day by day—as you begin to "see the light" in your plight to become the best employee that you know you were destined to be.

QUIZ
You might have a bad boss if . . .

This book is a tell-all tale of my real life experiences of having my good boss gone bad.

I've been fortunate to have had my share of good bosses. Unfortunately, I've encountered too many bad bosses as well. Some were downright evil, others pathological liars, and still other bad bosses just never got the memo on how to be a good boss. Not that *not* knowing how to be a good boss is an excuse; but it helps to better understand why work environments can be so unproductive and at times simply toxic.

The good news is knowing that there is a good side to having a bad boss. So, first let's examine some factors to make sure you are indeed working for/with a bad boss. Take a few minutes to review the following scenarios to determine whether your good boss has gone bad.

After you have completed the quiz below, the following chapters will further examine each scenario and discuss the positive points at which you can implement in an effort to empower yourself in your journey of survival and thriving at a workplace when a good boss goes bad. Here we go . . .

You might have a bad boss if:

1) The majority or only type of *communication* email or correspondence you receive from your boss is sporadic, darn near non-existent, or always negative, ex. "You're late!" or "What happened here?"

2) They only speak to you if/when they need you to do something, ex. resolve and/or research a matter they don't want to be bothered with.

3) When you discuss with them the importance of "work/ life balance" and their face goes blank and/or they start to suggest a new career path for you.

4) The only time you engage in eye contact with your boss is when you are actually speaking to them or when in a staff meeting (and it's your turn to speak).

5) You feel so detached that you don't even feel a need to speak to or follow up with your boss on matters. Or if/ when you do follow up, it's always by email—never face-to-face or even by phone. That way your boss cannot further engage you (like ask you to come to their office—right now).

6) The only time your boss gets excited is when the company is experiencing a sales gain or increase in

clientele (that makes them look good—on paper) or when they win a company award (which is just another plaque to go on their wall).

7) Your boss makes new changes and/or dictates a new process—from their chair (in *their* office). In reality, you know their idea will never work (because of their severe level of detachment and denial).

8) You can predict their every "canned" response or comment, ex.

    a. "How are you today?" (if they happen to run into you in the hallway).

    b. "How can we make this better?" (they only say this when in crisis mode, knowing you're the only one who can fix the problem. But actually they're implying "I want you to leave me alone now and go fix this problem quickly". Your boss doesn't really care how.

9) They stick to a scripted plan at meetings; never wavering because if they did they'd be lost and forced to actually "think off the cuff" and be truly engaging, which is not a strong skill set of a bad boss.

10) They really don't see that all is imploding around them—ex. no loyalty in their department, a "don't care" mentality amongst the general staff, morale of company is "in the tank", customer service scores are suffering, internal feedback is negative, etc.

Of course there are more instances, but these are just a few to help you better determine if you are indeed working for a bad boss or just a boss that is simply having a bad boss day (or week or month) or possibly experiencing a learning curve because they are new or adjusting to corporate changes.

Chapter 1

You might have a bad boss if . . .

The majority or only type of communication, email, or correspondence you receive from your boss is sporadic, darn near non-existent, or always negative, such as "You're late!" or "What happened here?"

Take a moment and think about how you mostly communicate (if at all) with your boss. During one of my former boss's demise, I can recall when communication came nearly to a halt, all but for emails. I don't know if my boss was intimidated by me, felt threatened since I was one of the most prepared managers, or knew that I saw through his level of incompetence when we met face-to-face.

I can recall with another former boss when we were supposed to have regularly scheduled weekly meetings. Not to say that I looked forward to meeting with my boss—I assure you I did not—but the fact that the meetings were requested meant I had to set aside additional time to be prepared to discuss (or more likely refute) whatever happened to be on his agenda. But here is where the "good" went "bad". In a course of 6 months, I'd say we officially met face-to-face only 3-4 times (and that's stretching it). How am I supposed to gauge my performance or know his realistic expectations if we meet either on a whim or casually at his leisure? Needless to say, my performance evaluations were never an adequate depiction of the depth of my true skills, talents, and abilities. How could they be if they were never assessed regularly?

GOOD BOSS: A good boss is aware of the importance of initiating, scheduling and holding meetings. The key here is consistency, even if they are not weekly.

BAD BOSS: After the 1st or 2nd meeting (which were still sporadic at that), the weekly meetings all but stopped. The meetings were either cancelled without notice (because my boss was not in the office) or rescheduled to "next week", but that never came because my boss would regularly be missing in action, never to be found in the office as scheduled.

For the few times we did meet, it was to point out problems in my department, sprinkled with a few "pats on the back". But the negative so far outweighed the positive, that whenever a meeting was requested, it was met with great dread on my part. More than not, the suggestions I made were either poorly supported or all but ignored and not valued.

YOUR PART: As an employee you must recognize that even though you/your talents are not valued, that you are a valuable part of an organization (this goes beyond what your boss says, thinks or feel). Knowing my worth helped me to keep my composure during times when I wanted to scream at the top of my lungs. Believing that I was where I needed to be caused me to still be a positive asset to my department as well as to my boss (inadvertently). If I did a good job, then my boss looked liked he did a good job (even if it was "just on paper").

A key lesson I learned from a former associate is to always document what was said or done, especially if in regards to your boss. See, regardless of the lack of communication on your boss's part, *you* must be proactive. Even though your boss is not communicating with you (because, frankly he just doesn't care) it doesn't mean that you can't "take charge" and hold him accountable by documenting each instance.

For example, if a meeting was "missed"; simply follow up with an email inquiry of the rescheduled meeting or list some ideas you had hoped to discuss with them at the scheduled meeting. This way, you are not blatantly blaming your boss for his incompetence, but instead, are showing you still value his input (whether you do or not) and are a team player (even though he is severely detached from his duties as your boss). Remember, it is not your role to tell or show your boss his dysfunction, but to merely hold him accountable to what he initiated, done in a non-threatening way. Even if your boss doesn't reply to your email (most of the time, he never will), you don't have to worry because *you* followed up and now have your proof.

FINAL THOUGHT: All in all, you must keep your wits about you, realizing it is all a game. But it still is very much a dog-eat-dog world out there. So don't get bitten (or bitter).

Instead, get better, and always remember to document. For more guidance on how to "play the game of life", consider career coaching with April at www.goodbossesgonebad.com.

Chapter 2

You might have a bad boss if . . .

He only speaks to you if/when he needs you to do something, ex. resolve and/or research a matter he doesn't want to be bothered with.

We've all been there. I'm sure you can pinpoint a time when you were given a task to complete when you knew good and well (or perhaps, realized after the fact) that your boss pawned off yet another assignment to you just so he could clear off his own desk a little quicker. I can recall many times when I stayed late, skipped or/shortened my lunch, or even needlessly placed my job above my children all in the name of being a team player to get the job done.

I distinctly remember a particular instance. Of course, we were at crunch time. Yet the responsibility squarely fell on my shoulders. As my boss waltzed out of the office, like clock work at 5pm, I half-heartedly smiled and secretly wished I could trade places with my boss. I sighed as the office silenced and began to get to work.

Let me take a moment to explain a deceptive workplace principle to you. As we so often do, we get tricked into believing "our day will come" when we can do the same as our boss—leave work early (or heck, even leave work on time for once). Unfortunately, some workplaces are so dysfunctional, where it seems as if there are never enough hours in a day to complete even the basic of tasks.

Many bad bosses are fully aware of this. Most are in denial of the toxic level of dysfunction. They rationalize "If I can get *my* work done, why can't you?" as they are the first person to leave the office each day (that is, if they even came in that day). But they have learned how to master the game of keeping "the help" occupied which allows them to "vacate the premises" on time or at their leisure. But in all fairness to you think of it like this. If they didn't think you were competent enough to complete the tasks they've delegated to you, then your boss wouldn't have given it to you.

GOOD BOSS: A good boss is confident enough in your skills to choose you to handle a particular situation or research a particular matter on his behalf.

BAD BOSS: Hindsight is 20:20, when you realize that you've been asked to resolve or complete a project that should/could have been handled by your bad boss. Unfortunately, delegation of even the basic of duties becomes a daily "to do" list for a bad boss.

YOUR PART: Now back to my moment of revelation. I was working late on a project that was due the next day. While under the wire, frantic and alone at night at the office *again*, I received a phone call from my former husband. He asked when I would be coming home. Frustrated and offended that he would even ask me that question, I snapped back at him "Soon, when my work is done!" Duh! Didn't he realize that he was interrupting me!? Well, I'll never forget the words that came out of his mouth next. He proudly informs me that I just missed my daughter taking her first steps. Now if you are a parent, you know that your child's first steps are a pivotal moment that will bring even the strongest of persons to tears. It is just one of those moments that you can never get back. Needless to say, at that point, my world stood still. I asked myself "What are you doing?" As I sat there looking at the documents on my desk, I calmly stood up, marked my spot with a stickie note, turned off my computer, and left. With every step to my car, I fought back tears of guilt tinged with a bit of jealousy (because I was a mom who missed this moment). I vowed to myself never to let this happen again.

It is amazing how unknowingly and innocently kids can help you quickly snap back into reality. Now, as a mother of three children, I sincerely believe that that is their God-given duty—to be a constant reminder to parents or guardians of the little things that really matter in life.

FINAL THOUGHT: Stay focused. Don't be a doormat. Instead, determine that your boss's constant delegation is an unintentional "method to his madness" that'll help you further develop in your career. So, be a champion for increased efficiency and team building. In all actuality, the delegated tasks are skill building opportunities affording you the "bragging rights" to either:

1) Present during your next performance review with your boss. This reminds as well as provides him with documented proof of your value and commitment to the department and company.

2) Mention your skills while at a future job interview, if you decide to leave your current job.

3) List on your updated resume as skills, duties and knowledge learned while employed. See, your boss doesn't even realize that in his quest to pawn off his responsibilities, he is preparing you for your next promotion. Since you're going to get stuck doing it anyway, make every dreaded delegation count.

Chapter 3

You might have a bad boss if . . .

When you discuss with him the importance of
"work/life balance" and his face goes blank and/or he
starts to suggest a new career path for you.

I can vividly recall a meeting I had once with a former boss. I had been wrestling with the thought of having to make a career change in order to better balance my single parent lifestyle. Having been a stay-at-home mom where my deadlines centered around my children, I also have been a career woman who juggled deadlines at the office just as well. But just like when Diane Keaton's character in the movie "Baby Boom" finally lets reality sink in that she no longer is the corporate "tiger lady" because she now has a child; I, too, had reached my limit of sacrificing too much to try to have it all.

GOOD BOSS: A good boss, when asked to meet, will honor your request to discuss what's on your mind. Even if your request is impromptu. Although I must admit, I have on a number of occasions actually popped into my boss's office and sat down before my request to meet could even be denied. This is a skill you learn to finesse as you get to know your boss—timing is essential.

BAD BOSS: During the meeting, I explained to my boss how I could no longer keep up the pace of what was required for the position. I made it very clear that it was not due to my inability to perform my duties, but more so due to an unrealistic work/life balance that my job duties required. But instead of my boss validating my value, commitment, and concern for the company, my boss offered little to no empathy or sympathy to my situation. This reaction further confirmed my decision to seek employment elsewhere. For many workplaces, we are in a time where companies are cutting costs and eliminating positions. This most likely means that the staff left behind inherits the duties of the now unfilled positions.

YOUR PART: As an employee, you must come to terms with this fact: It's not fair, but somebody's got to do it and that "somebody" will most likely be YOU. We all know it surely won't be your boss. In knowing this before hand, you must brace yourself for the blow. It's like knowing when riding a roller coaster that the big dip is coming up after the next big turn. So you brace yourself for the sinking feeling you are sure to experience in your stomach. So goes the same at the workplace (though some may relate this feeling to more like a sucker punch in the gut). Nevertheless, as more duties are piled on your plate (sorry, I mean as more duties are being needlessly delegated to you by your bad boss), it directly impacts your work/life balance. Gone are the days when you can skip out of the office with a smile on your face with the rest of your coworkers. You no longer whistle while you work, but instead grin and bear the brunt of having a bad boss. You now realize that a full hour's lunch is a thing of the past if you are going to beat your new deadlines. You begin to seriously question whether sleep is overrated. And you develop a new technique to being productive while functioning "on fumes" from a lack of rest. It is when you finally get a quiet moment (which most likely is during a bathroom break because you just couldn't "hold it" anymore), that you realize that you single handedly have taken the "rat race" to a whole new level. As the lyrics to the song "Take This Job and Shove It" quickly become your daily workplace theme song, you realize that something has got to give. The point is you must choose between either your work or your life.

FINAL THOUGHT: How do you make the right choice between your work and your life/health? You can't just leave your job nor can you throw caution to the wind when it comes to your lifestyle. You must develop a mindset that strives for a perfect balance between clarity and efficiency. Seek clarity (clear cut solutions) in an effort to successfully complete the duties you are expected to accomplish at the workplace all within an realistic time frame. Short version: Keep your wits about you at the workplace so you can enjoy your life *away* from the workplace with your family and friends.

Since you know your bad boss will delegate tasks to you, plan for it. I have become a master of efficiency, mostly from being a single parent. But I've learned how to apply this same time-saving skill to the workplace. I can't tell you how many times that with forethought and carefully calculated plans with my team, mixed with impeccable timing, that I have been able to survive the workplace even while reporting to a bad boss.

Chapter 4

You might have a bad boss if . . .

*The only time you engage in eye contact with your boss
is when he is actually speaking to you or when in a
staff meeting (and it's your turn to speak).*

Staff meetings can be the best time for impressing or interacting with your boss. But timing is crucial. See, the more you get to know your boss, the better you can predict his mood and management style. The better you can "read" him, the better your work environment can be. For instance, I had a former manager who would start management meetings with a movie review or a recap of what the managers did over the weekend. So, every Monday, you knew to have some sort of story to tell. The more interesting the story, the better your week went. Or if you happened to see the same movie, then you were able to bond a bit more. I'm not saying that this was right, but that's just how it was. On the other hand, I had another former boss who never held meetings with me. I managed my team by sheer intuition and instinct because it sure wasn't a case of leadership by example (because there was <u>no</u> example). The only time I met with my manager was when she caught me walking past her office. She would yell my name and call me back to her office only to hold an impromptu "catch up" meeting.

GOOD BOSS: In the first case of a good boss gone bad, during the meetings he would create a sense of "I care about you" (at least at the onset). Even though we all knew at any given point he would cut the casual talk short and "get down to business" (and sometimes berate us to the point that we wished we had called in sick), we still cherished the few precious moments of bonding and that put us all at ease, at least temporarily.

In the second scenario, all I can say is that at least I knew *she* knew my name. That in fact proved that she knew I existed—if not but to do the tasks she didn't want to do and then gladly delegate to me. But, here's the key—she had to catch me first; which is why I rarely walked past her office. For the few times that she did catch me, I either didn't know she was in the building or I was reading my mail and forgot that I was heading in the direction of her office. In those cases, I had to "suck it up" and pray that her ill-planned meetings had a purpose and were brief.

BAD BOSS: There is nothing worse than to report to a manager who you think doesn't value your time, skills, and abilities. In reference to the second scenario above, every time I was called to my boss's office it was met with much dread and misery with every step I *slowly* took. You know it's bad when the mere sound of someone's voice sends you into a downward spiral of regret (that you showed up for work that day). If it weren't for the security cameras right outside my office and/or the fire alarm on the door, I would've snuck out the building. I honestly considered this plan of escape on more than one occasion (now of course, you didn't hear that from me). But it would be hard to prove that it wasn't me (security cameras and all). Unfortunately, I had to return to work tomorrow, so why prolong the inevitable, right?!

YOUR PART: In the case of the "movie review" manager, he was pretty predictable. So, whether you watched your favorite show on TV or caught a flick at the local theater, be ready to talk about it. Perhaps your manager is a sports fanatic—be prepared to chime in the "locker room" discussion during the meeting. In the case of the "missing in action" manager, always make decisions based on what you feel *your boss* would expect. When in a situation on the front line (as most times you will be since bad bosses rarely leave their office), ask yourself "What would my boss say or do?" Recall the last time you were summoned to their office to discuss a situation. What expectations were discussed? How did your boss feel you could've handled it better? Now, keeping these points in mind, just do what they say do. Keep it simple. If they say "Take care of the customer", then that is what you do. Don't rationalize whether their perspective is right or wrong (of course, I'm not suggesting you take part in something unethical). But remember, they are the boss. So, ultimately it is their way or the highway. At least now, when a particular situation presents itself, you will be confident to respond as your boss would respond; therefore decreasing the need for senseless conversation with them after the fact.

FINAL THOUGHT: Increased workplace efficiency equates to knowing your boss' expectations (as skewed and unpredictable as they may be). When dealing with a "bad boss" you are challenged to find some sort of consistency in their *in*consistency. Let me put it another way. The more you can "predict" their incompetence, the better an employee you will be. So, be prepared. Anticipate your boss's next move. It really isn't that hard. Simply take the time to observe the habits (bad and good) of your boss. For the most part "bad bosses" are pretty predictable in their actions or words (or lack thereof). But really over time their irresponsibility becomes quite routine—you begin to expect it and plan accordingly.

Chapter 5

You might have a bad boss if . . .

You feel so detached that you don't even feel a need to speak to or follow up with your boss on matters. Or if/when you do follow up, it's always by email—never face-to-face or by phone. That way your boss cannot further engage you (like ask you to come to their office—right now).

It came to a point with one of my former bosses that the level of detachment was so severe that the only way for me to rationalize his existence was that he was there to fill a position or title. He merely kept a seat warm or an office occupied. He was definitely not there to fulfill the *actual* duties of his title, but just to walk around with the title boldly branded on his chest (and outside of his door, of course).

GOOD BOSS: A good boss, at least will reply to your email. In my case, when emailing my boss, I would receive an answer only if I titled it "Urgent". I knew this was the only way to get a timely response (or *any* response for that matter). Other than that, my emails were treated as "informational only" and I became conditioned to not expect a response at all.

BAD BOSS: The lack of interaction got so bad with one of my former bosses that even when I passed her office I didn't speak. Heck, I didn't even bother to quicken my pace or soften my steps. I didn't care. She knew (well, I think she knew) that her existence in my world didn't really matter. It wasn't intentional, but a matter of psychological survival (so I wouldn't snap). It came to a point where I realized that communicating with her drained my development instead of motivated me to be a better manager. She had forced me to cross the point of no return. So at this point, the level of communication with my boss was nearly "null and void" unless it required immediate attention or approval from upper management.

YOUR PART: The key here is to make sure your boss doesn't have "read receipt" selected on the emails they send to you. That way, you can safely say, "Oh, I didn't get it" if they inquire about your receipt or response (but most likely, they never will even ask). Also, should you choose to respond, always select "Reply to all" just in case they are being sneaky (which many bad bosses tend to be). Last but certainly not least, always select "bcc" to "blindly" send an email to yourself (work AND personal email address), especially if the subject matter could later incriminate you or if you'll need to refer to it to clear your name at a later date. Yes, it can get *that* serious! Workplace politics have soared to a higher level—now you know.

FINAL THOUGHT: When all is said and done, you must determine what level of communication you need to have with your boss in order to not have it "bite you in the butt" when it comes to your performance appraisal (well, that is if your boss ever discusses your performance with you). If you are confident in your duties and can correctly interpret your boss's expectations, then you can probably function well with little to no communication. But if you are new to your position or entering a new career field, then input is needed from your boss, at least initially. The key is to become an expert in cracking the code of silence. So see, in no time you will become an expert in both nonverbal communication (the "new" language of the workplace) as well as mind-reading (a 21st century job skill)—who knew?! Seriously, if your bad boss is severely non-responsive, seek out a mentor or career coach to strategically help guide your career before you consider jumping ship.

Chapter 6

You might have a bad boss if . . .

The only time your boss gets excited is when the company is experiencing a sales gain or increase in clientele (that makes him look good—on paper) or when he wins a company award (which is just another plaque to go on his wall).

I've always been a person who observes others and listens to the words that come out of someone's mouth before I make a judgment call about them. I can honestly say that I am a person who weighs more on the side of nonverbal language vs. having an actual conversation with someone. I can recall a time when a former boss won company recognition that included a plaque for her (sorry, I mean it was a plaque for *the efforts of people* at that location, that is). At this particular department meeting, she had gathered all the staff to announce her acceptance of this award. As I surveyed the room (remember, I am a master at decoding body language) the looks on the faces of the team members were priceless. The more the manager talked about her award, the more disengaged and less interested the team members became. Yet, the manager continued to "toot her own horn", seemingly unbeknownst to the nonverbal cues from her uncaptivated audience. I wish I could've heard the thoughts of some of the listeners—they would have been priceless as well. I almost busted out in laughter (ok, I didn't, but I did smirk a bit) because my boss just didn't get it. She was the only person in the room that was excited, yet she couldn't or wouldn't see that others were gazing off into the horizon, or had such emotionless looks plastered on their faces. This example is an extreme case where denial is detrimental to the development of a workplace.

GOOD BOSS: The good part is at least the boss *is* doing something right (even if in their own mind) in order to receive recognition from the company.

BAD BOSS: The bad part is that the recognition comes at the expense of all the frustrated employees who have to put up with the mind games, insensitivity, and sometimes blatant disregard for their well being on a daily basis.

YOUR PART: Grin and bear it. When all is said and done (and a lot is being said, believe me), the real credit due will be awarded to the one(s) who really gets the job done. We all know that upper management will receive the credit for a job well done. A bad boss will solely bask in all the glory and keep the plaque or certificate in her office. But, a good boss, understands this as well, and will share the wealth—of appreciation and recognition—with all those who helped her get to the level she's at. In the end, that's all the bad boss will have—the plaque or certificate. I've come to believe that no, it doesn't have to be lonely at the top as long as you remember, that it is not just about you. So, as you prepare to be a future leader, remember this point, so you will be able to share your moment of glory *with* your team, not in spite of them.

FINAL THOUGHT: Understand that your time will come. A bad boss can look good on paper only so long, until then something has got to give. For instance, perhaps during a critical moment a question will be asked or a situation will present itself, where clearly the boss has no clue in how to resolve it. Who are they gonna call? YOU. So you must "be on your p's and q's" and not get hung up on the fact that the boss is claiming all the praise. Yes, I say again, your time will come, so you must be ready for it—at all times.

Chapter 7

You might have a bad boss if . . .

Your boss makes new changes and/or dictates a new process—from his chair (in his office). In reality, you know his idea will never work (because of the level of detachment and denial) . . .

I can recall a workplace environment when the only type of direction received from my boss was by email, a phone call, or during a meeting. He rarely came to the department to get a better picture of how things flowed. Yet, he never failed to give his "two cents" worth of advice on how to make things better, especially when/if upper management was inquiring. I am a firm believer that the best way to learn is not solely by relying on textbook/class knowledge. Equally important is real-time, on-the-job training, as well. This can only be learned by getting up and out of the comforts of your office/chair.

GOOD BOSS: A good boss will at least attempt to take charge, offer suggestions and try to be a good boss some of the time (even if the decisions they make only make sense in their head).

BAD BOSS: But many bad bosses take charge from the comforts of their chair . . . in their office. This is yet another case of detachment. There's nothing more evident to tearing down workplace morale than a bad boss not being willing to roll up his sleeves and pitch in. Or when a bad boss is not willing to see "how the other half lives" (or in this case works). Unfortunately, the end result, of his well intended suggestion tends to mess up the flow in your department.

YOUR PART: Towards the end of one of my former job assignments, I became an expert on quickly determining what really matters. In the midst of the madness, I also became extremely efficient in realizing whether the mind games were a power play or simply a result of my boss being intensely incompetent. You too must learn how to master these two skills: efficiency and mastering mind games. If you are a recent graduate, the earlier you grasp these principles, the better. If you are a seasoned professional, the better you master these skills, the better you'll be able to see the crap when it's being slung at you. Over time you will learn very quickly how to duck and weave and miss many a bullet. Truth be told, it <u>will</u> become effortless, if practiced properly (trust me, I know). How? Because you will come to a point where something has got to give. Your sanity or your position—and honestly, you need both! Believe me, I've been there, done that, and have the certificates and had the stress level to prove it, too. You must set your own level of tolerance. Once you peak at that breaking point, you will be forced to operate within a new level of normalcy—amidst all the chaos that greets you every morning, personally spearheaded by your bad boss.

FINAL THOUGHT: Pick your battles to fight. Sometimes it is better to throw up the white flag early on or throw in the towel while you can still save face. But other times, you must stand your ground (for your team members and yourself) to prove your point and fight (not literally, I don't expect you to bust into your boss's office declaring "put 'em up, buster!"). But you must come to a point where you see through the mess and declare that it stops right here, right now, with you. I can't tell you what will work best for you at your workplace, but where there is a will, there definitely is a way. And that will be your challenge. Contact April at www.goodbossesgonebad.com take the challenge to create critical career moves to propel you to the next level!

Chapter 8

You might have a bad boss if . . .

You can predict their every "canned" response or comment:

- *ex. "How are you today?" (if they happen to run into you in the hallway).*

- *ex. "How can we make this better?" (they only say this when in crisis mode, knowing you're the only one who can fix the problem. But actually they're implying "I want you to leave me alone, go fix this problem quickly. (not really caring how you get it done).*

Workplace telepathy does exist (ok, not really). But a perfect example is when you can "predict" how your boss will respond to a situation. to a situation by your boss. I remember one former boss who when she (regretfully) greeted a supervisor she would always ask "How are you today?" I always thought about responding by saying "Do you *not* see the look of dread on my face?" But I admit most of the time, I just said "Fine!" or referred to the weather in an honest attempt to keep it moving. After a while, I learned which question or comment was a canned response and that in fact she really wasn't overly concerned about my department or me.

Another example is when your bad boss goes into crisis mode (usually to save his own butt, which in the end results in you getting caught up in the crap). I remember a former bad boss who would *magically appear* only when there was an opportunity to be seen or when his butt was on the line. This was the only time when others and myself would see him "roll up his sleeve" and actually pitch in. Unfortunately, the pitching in caused more problems after the fact. Take note, this is yet another true indication of a bad boss. Even after asking "How can we make this better?" a bad boss causes more mayhem in the aftermath of his so called assistance. It could get to the point of where you'd whether he sat in his office instead of trying to inject his input.

GOOD BOSS: A good boss can "talk the talk" with the best of them. Quite simply, that is why they *are* the boss. Their canned responses *seem* sincere and full of concern for your well being—at least on the surface.

BAD BOSS: The words coming out of the mouth of a bad boss usually are mixed messages. Though you hear him ask "How are you doing?" his intentions are not pure—most times they really don't care how you are doing and are not waiting for your honest response anyway. There is no true connection.

When a bad boss asks "How can we make this better?" most times their true motive is to get <u>YOU</u> to resolve the current situation. Then all he'll have to do is simply agree or disagree with your suggestion yet still be blameless because it wasn't his idea in the first place. Remember this the next time he pulls out his pen and paper while the both of you are sitting in his office. I can eerily recall an awkward moment of silence as the pressure was thrown back at me to resolve a situation that I clearly needed my boss's assistance on—hence, me contacting him. I've even had a bad boss who started responding to emails while waiting for me to resolve the situation. But remember, this is their perspective because bad bosses become so detached from how the rest of the office really operates (see Chapter 7). He really doesn't have a clue as to how to resolve the issue you are presenting to him.

YOUR PART: Determine when and how to engage your boss. Remember, these times will be few and far in between, so you've got to make each moment count. After a while you will come to know the interests, motives, and what motivates your bad boss. If appropriately assessed, then you will have the ear of your bad boss (if you want it). So be creative in developing your own scripted/canned responses. As you know, the timing is critical also.

FINAL THOUGHT: Realize that the moments of one-on-one engagement with your boss will be few and far in between. Since you recognize this, you've got to always be prepared with a canned response or comment that leaves a positive impression. You've got to make every moment count—literally, because you may have only 1-2 minutes as you pass each other in the hallway or before or after a meeting.

Now, remember those awkward moments I was referring to earlier? Use this time as a perfect opportunity to show your boss your value and commitment to them (gulp)! But more importantly, it shows your commitment to your team and the company. So go ahead and put on your thinking cap since you know your boss most likely won't provide much input. Come to the table (or actually, their desk) with suggestions of your own or agree to follow up with your boss—via email. Remember, document your ideas and suggestions, so they can't steal and claim it as their own.

Chapter 9

You might have a bad boss if . . .

*He sticks to a scripted plan at meetings; never wavering
because if he did he'd be lost and forced to actually
"think off the cuff" and be truly engaging; which is not
a strong skill set of a bad boss.*

Even in a controlled environment, disengagement can still be one of the most negative qualities found in a bad boss. I can recall during training sessions led by a former bad boss where every word was practically read from the provided script. Every pause was taken as suggested in the training materials (we knew this because we had the print out as well). My peers and I attended this training because it was focused on team building that was supposed to increase communication (something we all knew needed to be addressed). I believe that had any other facilitator been selected besides our bad boss, it would have been effective or at least a foundation at which to build. But unfortunately the bad boss was only interested in checking this off her "to do" list for the day. So, once again we left the so called team building training even more isolated, frustrated, and hopeless that any *real* changes would be made.

GOOD BOSS: Good bosses are intelligent enough to read and follow scripted training materials or relay a scripted message from a news release. They are also smart enough to schedule the training within the given time frames (even if it means bringing in the whole team at the "crack of dawn" on a Friday morning or having them stay later after working a full day).

BAD BOSS: Scripted plans and/or training materials are prime opportunities for a bad boss to bridge the gap, but most times he only ends up further widening the divide.

Bad bosses can not steer too far from the provided materials. It is their deepest fear, yet the stark reality, that everything will fall apart because they will be challenged to come up with original ideas because they are so disengaged (See chapter 1). Bad bosses tend not to think outside the box which stifles creativity and crushes the possibility of progress of a team or department.

YOUR PART: Don't beat your bad boss up too much even when you could have seized the opportunity to do so. Since we had the same materials in front of us, we could've easily planned a pre-empted strike at any time because we could've read ahead. I must admit that on a few occasions I have done this. But it was only after careful strategic planning on my part, because I was fully aware that there would be some backlash because after all, they are the boss. I do not suggest an "attack" unless you have calculated the costs vs. the benefits of doing so. If it seems as if it would be a move to better your career, then go for. But if there are too many unknown variables, do not proceed. Contact April for one-on-one consulting on critical career moves.

FINAL THOUGHT: Always be prepared to make a move or make a mark at the workplace. Most times it won't be hard to determine the best time to step out from the crowd because opportunities present themselves all the time. But with any decision you make, you must carefully and strategically weigh the pros vs. the cons. Then you must be focused enough to either see the plan through to the end or to abort and save face. Sometimes the decision will involve a subtle move, other times it will be bold enough for all to see and experience—including your bad boss. Depending on your plan of action, remember the best scenario is the one where both you and your bad boss agree to a win-win solution without threats, regrets, or remorse.

Chapter 10

You might have a bad boss if . . .

He really doesn't see that all is imploding around him—ex. no loyalty in their department, "don't care" mentality amongst the staff, morale of company is "in the tank", customer service scores are suffering, internal feedback is negative, etc.

This is the ultimate display of denial by a bad boss. He continues to grin, greet, and walk around like nothing is happening. You know he's read the customer comments. Even though the good outweigh the bad; the bad ones are still an indication that something is seriously wrong. You also know that beyond a shadow of a doubt your boss has read the internal comments made by employees that point a finger directly at him as the main culprit for the demise of the department.

GOOD BOSS: A good boss will "suck it up" and take the concerns expressed by those both externally and internally and use them constructively to move forward and make a change in the dynamics within the department.

BAD BOSS: A bad boss will continue to "bury their heads in the sand"; hoping that it'll all blow over and that ultimately no one will remember. The problem is that the sand will begin to suffocate and choke the life out of the boss. It will come to a point where they will have to throw out the life preserver, but unfortunately, no one will be there to pull them back in (not even the "brown noser", because they're not sure if they can withstand the backlash they'll endure from their peers).

YOUR PART: Many times, I've mentored young or newly hired managers on the principle to "duck and weave". The key here is to be observant; always on the lookout for clues and tips to what's going on in the workplace. There are always things said and/or done in the office, you just have to be aware of them especially if they are nonverbal clues. In today's workplace, many times the internal insurrection will be unheard or unseen until it happens. Know that the strategic plotting and premeditated plans are in existence. In fact, if you look closely, you'll sense the calm before the storm.

FINAL THOUGHT: I've learned from many mentors (both current and past) how to survive while working in toxic environments. It is a skill that cannot be read about in a book or taught in a single college course. It can only be truly mastered through on-the-job-training. You must be in the trenches to truly experience and live to tell the tale of how insane some of today's workplaces really are. I could go on and on of many more workplace horror stories that occurred, but you'd have to have been there to believe me. But even in the midst of the madness of reporting to a bad boss, only the strong learn to endure, occasionally "duck and weave", only to ultimately rise above the mess. Which one will you be? Will you cave and fold under the pressure or will you stand strong and be a survivor? The choice is yours.

Bonus "Good Bosses Gone Bad" tips

Tip #1: Lingering issues with no resolution. One of the greatest impediments to workplace progress is the lack of the sense of urgency in quickly resolving matters.

A good boss will seize the opportunity to "save the day" or "fall on the sword" in order to be the one to bear the burden of addressing and resolving a workplace problem.

A bad boss will go straight into denial mode and act as if the issue doesn't exist. I've also seen bad bosses who will simply try to pacify the problem. Oh, they'll "address" the issue—lightly—careful not to make too much a fuss about it. But will give just enough attention to it to appear as if they are addressing the issue.

Ultimately, the burden of resolving the issue will fall upon the shoulders of the person who brought it to the attention of the bad boss. The bad boss believes that since an employee brought it up, then they should find a solution to it. So, as you present the issue, be prepared to offer a solution as well. It could quite possibly become a valued skill set and/or achievement to add to your resume.

Tip #2: Consistent incompetence.

A good boss will accept that they are not at the level where they need to be. A good boss will know that there is honor in this acknowledgment. So, with that being said, their department will be glad to come to the table and work with them.

It never fails to amaze me how bad bosses misjudge their own level of incompetence. I keep thinking surely in their quiet moments; when they look in the mirror and reflect on their day, does a bad boss *not* see how their consistent incompetence is chipping away at the foundation of the company or their own department? But I guess the fact that I'm writing this book, clearly answers my question—NO, they do not!

So, if a bad boss chooses to not recognize that their consistent incompetence is draining the department, what are you to do? Once again, this is a perfect opportunity to turn a bad situation into a resume builder opportunity. First, see where the loopholes exist. Next, determine where you can best make an impact and lasting impression (even after you are long gone). Last, but certainly not least, make sure you document your initial suggestion and all following input. Never verbally suggest an idea to a bad boss. You already know credit will not be given where credit is due—document, document, document.

Tip #3: Learned behavior from a bad boss.

Two types of "bad boss" learned behaviors that I personally have had to challenge myself to not adopt are 1) detachment from your department and 2) a checklist mentality.

Detachment from your department slowly seeps in as the pride and joy of being a leader in your department is stolen from you each day you are forced to interact with your own bad boss (the king/queen of detachment). You are faced with the "catch-22" of sincerely caring for your department while reporting to a bad boss who doesn't care about anything except their status.

A checklist mentality further creates an environment of detachment because the bad boss rationalizes that they are "good" because at the end of the day his "to-do's" are all checked off on his checklist. But the question is "Has he really done anything today?" Well according to the bad boss, "Yes!" But in the minds of those who report to the bad boss, it is a resounding "No!"

Good bosses are able to immediately recognize and address these negative behaviors they exhibit. They do this not to embarrass themselves, but so the negative behaviors are not engrained into the mindset of future leaders currently within the workplace and/or so the morale of the workplace doesn't get too negative.

Bad bosses could care less about the morale of those who report to them. As long as they are still in control and have people at their beck and call they can still keep their heads above water as they leave every day at 5pm and enjoy a full weekend off.

The checklist mentality is a dangerous gauge that bad bosses use to determine their own performance level. The fallacy occurs when their perception is so skewed because they are the only judge and are a one-person jury.

At the end of the day, you have to challenge yourself not to fall trap to these two learned behaviors. I know it may be hard at times because you tend to become like those who are around you. But you must take a step back and see past the mirage of how the life of a bad boss truly is. I can in fact say that in the case of a bad boss, it *is* lonely at the top. I know this by observing how many countless days my former bad bosses have sat at their desk eating their lunch—alone or have called an informal meeting at their home or other offsite area only for it to be poorly attended.

About April Boyd-Noronha

April Boyd-Noronha, MBA, is an advocate for employees who seem to have lost hope as members of today's workforce. Highly respected as a leading trainer and consultant in the customer service and retail industry, her expertise is drawn from her own experiences of survival within toxic workplaces under the leadership of bad bosses. April is committed to sharing her insights, reflections, and revelations to empower today's frustrated "working poor" and even the seasoned professionals who have been forced to re-enter today's workplace. She brings a wealth of experience from a career that spans from self-employed educational consultant, TV/radio show host & executive producer, youth advocate, higher education administrator, customer service manager, and even a bid as a local school board candidate. April consults clients on critical career moves as retail trainer expert at her company *www.TheRetailTrainer.com*. She teaches workplace relations courses as adjunct faculty through the University of Missouri-Kansas City's Communiversity program. April is Chief Blogger at *www.SingleParentLiving.net* where she tells of her transition from stay-at-home mom to sole provider of three children.

To correspond with April Boyd-Noronha, write to:

The Retail Trainer
P.O. Box 7008
Lee's Summit, MO 64064

Email her at april@theretailtrainer.com
or log on to her websites:
www.theretailtrainer.com
www.goodbossesgonebad.com
www.singleparentliving.net

For information on booking her for
a speaking engagement, call
1-816-214-3717
or log on to www.theretailtrainer.com

www.ingramcontent.com/pod-product-compliance
Lightning Source LLC
Chambersburg PA
CBHW021251280526
45784CB00005B/2332